the BIG ONE LINE A DAY JOURNAL for MOMS

5 YEARS OF DAILY REFLECTIONS
AND MEMORIES

ROCKRIDGE
PRESS

For general information on our other products and
services, please contact our Customer Care Depart-
ment within the United States at (866) 744-2665, or
outside the United States at (510) 253-0500.

Hardcover ISBN: 978-1-68539-696-1
Paperback ISBN: 978-1-68539-695-4

Manufactured in the United States of America

Interior and Cover Designer: Jami Spittler
Graphic Designer: J.A. Mäger
Art Producer: Melissa Malinowsky
Editor: Carolyn Abate
Production Editor: Dylan Julian
Production Manager: Holly Haydash

Illustrations © burlapandlace/Creative Market, pp.
cover, i, iv, v; All other illustrations used under license
from Shutterstock.com

10 9 8 7 6 5 4 3 2 1 0

This Journal Belongs To:

....

INTRODUCTION

Hello! Welcome to your very own five-year journal. It was created with you in mind: a busy mom, with lots of responsibilities. It's no secret that daily life can get very hectic, very quickly. Between taking care of your family, your children, your household, and your job, the responsibilities add up!

The days can go by so quickly that the idea of carving out a moment to reflect about what you experienced or noticed on any given day may seem next to impossible. That's where this journal comes in handy. Inside these pages, you can record your daily memories for up to five years. Spending just a few minutes each day with this journal gives you the chance to write down your unique thoughts and experiences. Write about your relationship with your spouse or partner, your children, your parents or siblings, your neighbors or friends, your experiences at work, where you volunteer, or your place of worship. Whatever comes to mind.

The best part is that this journal meets you where you are—you can begin on whatever day you wish. But don't forget to record the year! Then, at the end of any given year, you can just keep going into the next one. Continue until you've filled up these pages with five years of memories.

When all is said and done, you'll have more than 1,800 days of life experiences to look back on in wonder and awe. So whether you write in this journal first thing every morning, right before you go to sleep, or in the middle of making dinner, remember that this is your time. So please make the most of it.

JANUARY

JANUARY

1

20 _____ _____

_____

20 _____ _____

_____

20 _____ _____

_____

20 _____ _____

_____

20 _____ _____

_____

2

20 _____ _____

_____

20 _____ _____

_____

20 _____ _____

_____

20 _____ _____

_____

20 _____ _____

_____

20...... _____

_____

20...... _____

_____

3 20...... _____

_____

20...... _____

_____

20...... _____

_____

20...... _____

_____

20...... _____

_____

4 20...... _____

_____

20...... _____

_____

20...... _____

_____

JANUARY

20_____ _____
         _____

20_____ _____
         _____

5 20_____ _____
              _____

20_____ _____
         _____

20_____ _____
         _____

20_____ _____
         _____

20_____ _____
         _____

6 20_____ _____
              _____

20_____ _____
         _____

20_____ _____
         _____

7

20 _____ _____

20 _____ _____

20 _____ _____

20 _____ _____

20 _____ _____

8

20 _____ _____

20 _____ _____

20 _____ _____

20 _____ _____

20 _____ _____

JANUARY

9

20 _____
_____
20 _____
20 _____
_____
20 _____
_____
20 _____
_____

10

20 _____
_____
20 _____
_____
20 _____
_____
20 _____
_____
20 _____
_____

11 20......

20......

20......

20......

20......

20......

20......

20......

12 20......

20......

20......

JANUARY

20 _____ _____

_____

20 _____ _____

_____

13 20 _____ _____

_____

20 _____ _____

_____

20 _____ _____

_____

20 _____ _____

_____

20 _____ _____

_____

14 20 _____ _____

_____

20 _____ _____

_____

20 _____ _____

_____

20 _____

20 _____

15 20 _____

20 _____

20 _____

20 _____

20 _____

16 20 _____

20 _____

20 _____

JANUARY

20 _____

20 _____

17 20 _____

20 _____

20 _____

20 _____

20 _____

18 20 _____

20 _____

20 _____

20...... _____

20...... _____

19 **20**...... _____

20...... _____

20...... _____

20...... _____

20...... _____

20 **20**...... _____

20...... _____

20...... _____

JANUARY

21

20 ___ _____

20 ___ _____

20 ___ _____

20 ___ _____

20 ___ _____

22

20 ___ _____

20 ___ _____

20 ___ _____

20 ___ _____

20 ___ _____

23

20...... _____
_____
20...... _____
_____
20...... _____
_____
20...... _____
_____
20...... _____
_____

24

20...... _____
_____
20...... _____
_____
20...... _____
_____
20...... _____
_____
20...... _____
_____

JANUARY

20____ _____
_____
20____ _____
_____
25 20____ _____
_____
20____ _____
_____
20____ _____
_____

20____ _____
_____
20____ _____
_____
26 20____ _____
_____
20____ _____
_____
20____ _____
_____

27

20...... _____

20...... _____

20...... _____

20...... _____

20...... _____

28

20...... _____

20...... _____

20...... _____

20...... _____

20...... _____

JANUARY

20___ _____
_____
_____
29 20___ _____
_____
20___ _____
_____
20___ _____
_____

20___ _____
_____
20___ _____
_____
30 20___ _____
_____
20___ _____
_____
20___ _____
_____

31

20...... _____

20...... _____

20...... _____

20...... _____

20...... _____

FEBRUARY

FEBRUARY

20......

20......

1 20......

20......

20......

20......

20......

2 20......

20......

20......

20_____

20_____

3 20_____

20_____

20_____

20_____

20_____

4 20_____

20_____

20_____

FEBRUARY

20...... _____

20...... _____

5 20...... _____

20...... _____

20...... _____

20...... _____

20...... _____

6 20...... _____

20...... _____

20...... _____

7

20......

20......

20......

20......

20......

20......

8

20......

20......

20......

20......

20......

23

FEBRUARY

20...... _____
_____

20...... _____
_____

9 20...... _____
_____

20...... _____
_____

20...... _____
_____

20...... _____
_____

20...... _____
_____

10 20...... _____
_____

20...... _____
_____

20...... _____
_____

11

20......

20......

20......

20......

20......

12

20......

20......

20......

20......

20......

FEBRUARY

20...... _____
          _____

20...... _____
          _____

13 20...... _____
          _____

20...... _____
          _____

20...... _____
          _____

20...... _____
          _____

20...... _____
          _____

14 20...... _____
          _____

20...... _____
          _____

20...... _____
          _____

15 20......

20......

20......

20......

20......

20......

16 20......

20......

20......

20......

20......

FEBRUARY

17

20......
20......
20......
20......
20......

18

20......
20......
20......
20......
20......

20...... _____

20...... _____
         _____

19 20...... _____
         _____

20...... _____
         _____

20...... _____
         _____

20...... _____
         _____

20...... _____
         _____

20 20...... _____
         _____

20...... _____
         _____

20...... _____
         _____

FEBRUARY

20...... _____

20...... _____

21 20...... _____

20...... _____

20...... _____

20...... _____

20...... _____

22 20...... _____

20...... _____

20...... _____

23

20......

20......

20......

20......

20......

24

20......

20......

20......

20......

20......

FEBRUARY

20......

20......

25 20......

20......

20......

20......

20......

26 20......

20......

20......

27 20......

20......

20......

20......

20......

20......

20......

20......

20......

33

FEBRUARY

20..... _____
_____
20..... _____
_____
29 20..... _____
_____
20..... _____
_____
20..... _____
_____

MARCH

20......

20......

| 20......

20......

20......

2 20......

20......

20......

20......

3

20...... _____

_____

20...... _____

_____

20...... _____

_____

20...... _____

_____

20...... _____

_____

20...... _____

_____

20...... _____

_____

4

20...... _____

_____

20...... _____

_____

20...... _____

_____

MARCH

5

20......

20......

20......

20......

20......

6

20......

20......

20......

20......

20......

40

20...... _____

20...... _____

7 20...... _____

20...... _____

20...... _____

20...... _____

20...... _____

8 20...... _____

20...... _____

20...... _____

MARCH

20...... _____
_____

20...... _____
_____

9 20...... _____
_____

20...... _____
_____

20...... _____
_____

20...... _____
_____

20...... _____
_____

10 20...... _____
_____

20...... _____
_____

20...... _____
_____

20...... _____

20...... _____

|| 20...... _____

20...... _____

20...... _____

20...... _____

20...... _____

|2 20...... _____

20...... _____

20...... _____

MARCH

20...... _____

20...... _____

13 20...... _____

20...... _____

20...... _____

20...... _____

20...... _____

14 20...... _____

20...... _____

20...... _____

20......

20......

15 20......

20......

20......

20......

20......

20......

16 20......

20......

20......

45

MARCH

17

20...... _____
_____
20...... _____
_____
20...... _____
_____
20...... _____
_____
20...... _____
_____

18

20...... _____
_____
20...... _____
_____
20...... _____
_____
20...... _____
_____
20...... _____
_____

19

20...... _____

20...... _____

20...... _____

20...... _____

20...... _____

20

20...... _____

20...... _____

20...... _____

20...... _____

20...... _____

MARCH

21

20...... _____
 _____
20...... _____
 _____
20...... _____
 _____
20...... _____
 _____
20...... _____
 _____

20...... _____
 _____
20...... _____
 _____

22

20...... _____
 _____
20...... _____
 _____
20...... _____
 _____

20...... _____

20...... _____

23 20...... _____

20...... _____

20...... _____

20...... _____

20...... _____

24 20...... _____

20...... _____

20...... _____

MARCH

20...... _____

20...... _____

25 20...... _____

20...... _____

20...... _____

20...... _____

20...... _____

26 20...... _____

20...... _____

20...... _____

27

20......

20......

20......

20......

20......

28

20......

20......

20......

20......

20......

MARCH

20...... _____
          _____
20...... _____
          _____
29 20...... _____
          _____
20...... _____
          _____
20...... _____
          _____

20...... _____
          _____
20...... _____
          _____
30 20...... _____
          _____
20...... _____
          _____
20...... _____
          _____

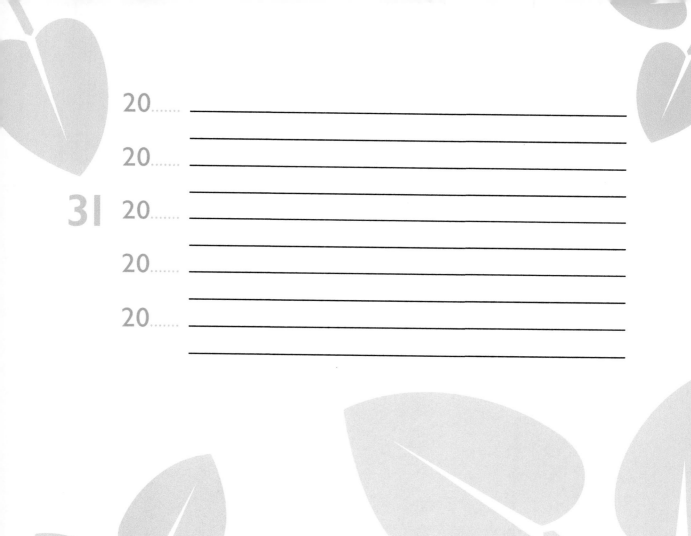

31

20......

20......

20......

20......

20......

APRIL

APRIL

20......

20......

1 20......

20......

20......

20......

20......

20......

2 20......

20......

20......

20...... _____

20...... _____

3 20...... _____

20...... _____

20...... _____

20...... _____

20...... _____

4 20...... _____

20...... _____

20...... _____

APRIL

20......

20......

5 20......

20......

20......

20......

20......

6 20......

20......

20......

20...... _____
        _____
20...... _____
        _____
7 20...... _____
        _____
20...... _____
        _____
20...... _____
        _____

20...... _____
        _____
20...... _____
        _____
8 20...... _____
        _____
20...... _____
        _____
20...... _____
        _____

APRIL

20...... _____
        _____
20...... _____
        _____
9 20...... _____
        _____
20...... _____
        _____
20...... _____
        _____

20...... _____
        _____
20...... _____
        _____
10 20...... _____
        _____
20...... _____
        _____
20...... _____
        _____

11

20...... _____
       _____
20...... _____
       _____
20...... _____
       _____
20...... _____
       _____
20...... _____
       _____

20...... _____
       _____
20...... _____
       _____
12 20...... _____
       _____
20...... _____
       _____
20...... _____
       _____

20......

20......

13 20......

20......

20......

20......

20......

14 20......

20......

20......

15   20......

20......

20......

20......

20......

16   20......

20......

20......

20......

20......

APRIL

20...... _____
          _____
20...... _____
          _____
17 20...... _____
          _____
20...... _____
          _____
20...... _____
          _____

20...... _____
          _____
20...... _____
          _____
18 20...... _____
          _____
20...... _____
          _____
20...... _____
          _____

19

20...... _____

20...... _____

20...... _____

20...... _____

20...... _____

20...... _____

20...... _____

20...... _____

20...... _____

20

20...... _____

20...... _____

APRIL

21

22

23

20......

20......

20......

20......

20......

20......

20......

20......

24

20......

20......

20......

APRIL

20...... _____

_____

20...... _____

_____

25 20...... _____

_____

20...... _____

_____

20...... _____

_____

20...... _____

_____

20...... _____

_____

26 20...... _____

_____

20...... _____

_____

20...... _____

_____

27

20......

20......

20......

20......

20......

28

20......

20......

20......

20......

20......

20......

20......

29 20......

20......

20......

20......

20......

30 20......

20......

20......

MAY

1

20...... _____

_____

20...... _____

_____

20...... _____

_____

20...... _____

_____

20...... _____

_____

2

20...... _____

_____

20...... _____

_____

20...... _____

_____

20...... _____

_____

20...... _____

_____

20...... _____
          _____
20...... _____
          _____
3 20...... _____
          _____
20...... _____
          _____
20...... _____
          _____

20...... _____
          _____
20...... _____
          _____
4 20...... _____
          _____
20...... _____
          _____
20...... _____
          _____

MAY

20...... _____
          _____
20...... _____
          _____
5 20...... _____
          _____
20...... _____
          _____
20...... _____
          _____

20...... _____
          _____
20...... _____
          _____
6 20...... _____
          _____
20...... _____
          _____
20...... _____
          _____

7 20......

20......

20......

20......

20......

20......

8 20......

20......

20......

20......

20......

20...... _____
          _____
20...... _____
          _____
9 20...... _____
          _____
20...... _____
          _____
20...... _____
          _____

20...... _____
          _____
20...... _____
          _____
10 20...... _____
          _____
20...... _____
          _____
20...... _____
          _____

11

20...... _____
_____
20...... _____
_____
20...... _____
_____
20...... _____
_____
20...... _____
_____

20...... _____
_____
20...... _____
_____
12 20...... _____
_____
20...... _____
_____
20...... _____
_____

20......

20......

13 20......

20......

20......

20......

20......

14 20......

20......

20......

15

20...... _____

20...... _____

20...... _____

20...... _____

20...... _____

20...... _____

20...... _____

20...... _____

16

20...... _____

20...... _____

20...... _____

20...... _____
_____

20...... _____
_____

17 20...... _____
_____

20...... _____
_____

20...... _____
_____

20...... _____
_____

20...... _____
_____

18 20...... _____
_____

20...... _____
_____

20...... _____
_____

19

20...... _____

20...... _____

20...... _____

20...... _____

20...... _____

20

20...... _____

20...... _____

20...... _____

20...... _____

20...... _____

MAY

21

20......

20......

20......

20......

20......

22

20......

20......

20......

20......

20......

23

20......

20......

20......

20......

20......

24

20......

20......

20......

20......

20......

20......

20......

25 20......

20......

20......

20......

20......

26 20......

20......

20......

27

20......

20......

20......

20......

20......

20......

28

20......

20......

20......

20......

20......

MAY

20......

20......

29 20......

20......

20......

20......

20......

30 20......

20......

20......

31

20......
_____
_____
20......
_____
_____
20......
_____
_____
20......
_____
_____
20......
_____
_____

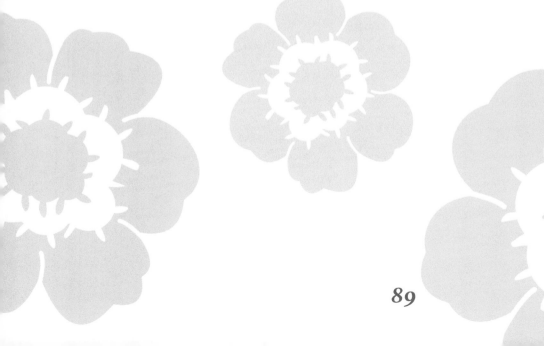

JUNE

JUNE

20...... _____
_____

20...... _____
_____

1 20...... _____
_____

20...... _____
_____

20...... _____
_____

20...... _____
_____

20...... _____
_____

2 20...... _____
_____

20...... _____
_____

20...... _____
_____

20...... _____

_____

20...... _____

_____

3 20...... _____

_____

20...... _____

_____

20...... _____

_____

20...... _____

_____

20...... _____

_____

4 20...... _____

_____

20...... _____

_____

20...... _____

_____

JUNE

5

20......

20......

20......

20......

20......

6

20......

20......

20......

20......

20......

7

20...... _____

20...... _____

20...... _____

20...... _____

20...... _____

20...... _____

20...... _____

8

20...... _____

20...... _____

20...... _____

JUNE

20...... _____
_____

20...... _____
_____

9 20...... _____
_____

20...... _____
_____

20...... _____
_____

20...... _____
_____

20...... _____
_____

10 20...... _____
_____

20...... _____
_____

20...... _____
_____

11

20......

20......

20......

20......

20......

12

20......

20......

20......

20......

20......

JUNE

13

20......

20......

20......

20......

20......

14

20......

20......

20......

20......

20......

15

20......

20......

20......

20......

20......

16

20......

20......

20......

20......

20......

JUNE

20...... _____

20...... _____

17 20...... _____

20...... _____

20...... _____

20...... _____

20...... _____

18 20...... _____

20...... _____

20...... _____

19 20......

20......

20......

20......

20......

20......

20 20......

20......

20......

20......

20......

JUNE

21

22

20......

20......

20......

20......

20......

20......

20......

20......

20......

20......

23

20......

20......

20......

20......

20......

24

20......

20......

20......

20......

20......

JUNE

20...... _____
_____

20...... _____
_____

25 20...... _____
_____

20...... _____
_____

20...... _____
_____

20...... _____
_____

20...... _____
_____

26 20...... _____
_____

20...... _____
_____

20...... _____
_____

27

20......

20......

20......

20......

20......

28

20......

20......

20......

20......

20......

JUNE

29

20......

20......

20......

20......

20......

30

20......

20......

20......

20......

20......

JULY

JULY

20...... _____
        _____
20...... _____
        _____
1 20...... _____
        _____
20...... _____
        _____
20...... _____
        _____

20...... _____
        _____
20...... _____
        _____
2 20...... _____
        _____
20...... _____
        _____
20...... _____
        _____

20...... _____

20...... _____

3 20...... _____

20...... _____

20...... _____

20...... _____

20...... _____

4 20...... _____

20...... _____

20...... _____

JULY

20...... _____
          _____
20...... _____
          _____
5 20...... _____
          _____
20...... _____
          _____
20...... _____
          _____

20...... _____
          _____
20...... _____
          _____
6 20...... _____
          _____
20...... _____
          _____
20...... _____
          _____

7

20...... _____

_____

20...... _____

_____

20...... _____

_____

20...... _____

_____

20...... _____

_____

20...... _____

_____

20...... _____

_____

8

20...... _____

_____

20...... _____

_____

20...... _____

_____

JULY

20...... _____
          _____
20...... _____
          _____
9 20...... _____
          _____
20...... _____
          _____
20...... _____
          _____

20...... _____
          _____
20...... _____
          _____
10 20...... _____
          _____
20...... _____
          _____
20...... _____
          _____

11

20...... _____
_____
20...... _____
_____
20...... _____
_____
20...... _____
_____
20...... _____
_____

20...... _____
_____
20...... _____
_____

12

20...... _____
_____
20...... _____
_____
20...... _____
_____

JULY

20...... _____
          _____

20...... _____
          _____

13 20...... _____
          _____

20...... _____
          _____

20...... _____
          _____

20...... _____
          _____

20...... _____
          _____

14 20...... _____
          _____

20...... _____
          _____

20...... _____
          _____

15 20......

20......

20......

20......

20......

16 20......

20......

20......

20......

20......

JULY

20...... _____
        _____
20...... _____
        _____
17 20...... _____
        _____
20...... _____
        _____
20...... _____
        _____

20...... _____
        _____
20...... _____
        _____
18 20...... _____
        _____
20...... _____
        _____
20...... _____
        _____

20...... _____

20...... _____

19 20...... _____

20...... _____

20...... _____

20...... _____

20...... _____

20 20...... _____

20...... _____

20...... _____

JULY

20......

20......

21 20......

20......

20......

20......

20......

22 20......

20......

20......

23

20......

20......

20......

20......

20......

20......

20......

20......

24

20......

20......

20......

JULY

20...... _____

20...... _____

25 20...... _____

20...... _____

20...... _____

20...... _____

20...... _____

26 20...... _____

20...... _____

20...... _____

20...... _____
         _____
20...... _____
27 20...... _____
         _____
20...... _____
         _____
20...... _____
         _____

20...... _____
         _____
20...... _____
         _____
28 20...... _____
         _____
20...... _____
         _____
20...... _____
         _____

20...... _____

20...... _____

29 20...... _____

20...... _____

20...... _____

20...... _____

20...... _____

30 20...... _____

20...... _____

20...... _____

31

20......

20......

20......

20......

20......

AUGUST

AUGUST

20...... _____
         _____
20...... _____
         _____
| 20...... _____
         _____
20...... _____
         _____
20...... _____
         _____
20...... _____
         _____

20...... _____
         _____
20...... _____
         _____
2 20...... _____
         _____
20...... _____
         _____
20...... _____
         _____

20...... _____

        _____

20...... _____

        _____

3 20...... _____

        _____

20...... _____

        _____

20...... _____

        _____

20...... _____

        _____

20...... _____

        _____

4 20...... _____

        _____

20...... _____

        _____

20...... _____

        _____

AUGUST

20...... _____
          _____
20...... _____
          _____
5 20...... _____
          _____
20...... _____
          _____
20...... _____
          _____

20...... _____
          _____
20...... _____
          _____
6 20...... _____
          _____
20...... _____
          _____
20...... _____
          _____

7

20......

20......

20......

20......

20......

8

20......

20......

20......

20......

20......

AUGUST

20......

20......

9 20......

20......

20......

20......

20......

10 20......

20......

20......

11

20......

20......

20......

20......

20......

12

20......

20......

20......

20......

20......

AUGUST

13

20...... _____
          _____
20...... _____
          _____
20...... _____
          _____
20...... _____
          _____
20...... _____
          _____

14

20...... _____
          _____
20...... _____
          _____
20...... _____
          _____
20...... _____
          _____
20...... _____
          _____

15

20......

20......

20......

20......

20......

16

20......

20......

20......

20......

20......

AUGUST

20...... _____

20...... _____

17 20...... _____

20...... _____

20...... _____

20...... _____

20...... _____

18 20...... _____

20...... _____

20...... _____

19

20......

20......

20......

20......

20......

20

20......

20......

20......

20......

20......

AUGUST

21

22

20......

20......

20......

20......

20......

20......

20......

20......

23 20......

20......

20......

20......

20......

20......

20......

20......

24 20......

20......

20......

AUGUST

20...... _____

20...... _____

25 20...... _____

20...... _____

20...... _____

20...... _____

20...... _____

26 20...... _____

20...... _____

20...... _____

27

20......

20......

20......

20......

20......

28

20......

20......

20......

20......

20......

AUGUST

20......

20......

29 20......

20......

20......

20......

20......

30 20......

20......

20......

31

20...... _____
          _____
20...... _____
          _____
20...... _____
          _____
20...... _____
          _____
20...... _____
          _____

SEPTEMBER

SEPTEMBER

20...... _____

20...... _____

1 20...... _____

20...... _____

20...... _____

20...... _____

20...... _____

2 20...... _____

20...... _____

20...... _____

20 _____

20 _____

3 20 _____

20 _____

20 _____

20 _____

20 _____

4 20 _____

20 _____

20 _____

SEPTEMBER

20...... _____
       _____

20...... _____
       _____

5 20...... _____
       _____

20...... _____
       _____

20...... _____
       _____

20...... _____
       _____

20...... _____
       _____

6 20...... _____
       _____

20...... _____
       _____

20...... _____
       _____

7 20......

20......

20......

20......

20......

20......

8 20......

20......

20......

20......

20......

SEPTEMBER

9

20......

20......

20......

20......

20......

10

20......

20......

20......

20......

20......

11

20......

20......

20......

20......

20......

20......

12

20......

20......

20......

20......

20......

SEPTEMBER

20___ _____
_____

20___ _____
_____

13 20___ _____
_____

20___ _____
_____

20___ _____
_____

20___ _____
_____

20___ _____
_____

14 20___ _____
_____

20___ _____
_____

20___ _____
_____

15

20......

20......

20......

20......

20......

16

20......

20......

20......

20......

20......

SEPTEMBER

20......

20......

17 20......

20......

20......

20......

20......

18 20......

20......

20......

19 20.....

20.....

20.....

20.....

20.....

20 20.....

20.....

20.....

20.....

20.....

SEPTEMBER

21

20 _____
20 _____
20 _____
20 _____
20 _____

22

20 _____
20 _____
20 _____
20 _____
20 _____

23

20......

20......

20......

20......

20......

24

20......

20......

20......

20......

20......

SEPTEMBER

20

20

25 20

20

20

20

20

26 20

20

20

27

20......

20......

20......

20......

20......

28

20......

20......

20......

20......

20......

SEPTEMBER

20....... _____
    _____
20....... _____
    _____
29 20....... _____
    _____
20....... _____
    _____
20....... _____
    _____

20....... _____
    _____
20....... _____
    _____
30 20....... _____
    _____
20....... _____
    _____
20....... _____
    _____

OCTOBER

OCTOBER

20...... _____
_____
20...... _____
_____
1 20...... _____
_____
20...... _____
_____
20...... _____
_____

20...... _____
_____
20...... _____
_____
2 20...... _____
_____
20...... _____
_____
20...... _____
_____

20...... _____
_____

20...... _____
_____

3 20...... _____
_____

20...... _____
_____

20...... _____
_____

20...... _____
_____

20...... _____
_____

4 20...... _____
_____

20...... _____
_____

20...... _____
_____

20...... _____

20...... _____

5 20...... _____

20...... _____

20...... _____

20...... _____

20...... _____

6 20...... _____

20...... _____

20...... _____

7

20...... _____
         _____
20...... _____
         _____
20...... _____
         _____
20...... _____
         _____
20...... _____
         _____

8

20...... _____
         _____
20...... _____
         _____
20...... _____
         _____
20...... _____
         _____
20...... _____
         _____

OCTOBER

9

20...... _____
_____
20...... _____
_____
20...... _____
_____
20...... _____
_____
20...... _____
_____

10

20...... _____
_____
20...... _____
_____
20...... _____
_____
20...... _____
_____
20...... _____
_____

11

20......

20......

20......

20......

20......

12

20......

20......

20......

20......

20......

OCTOBER

20...... _____
         _____

20...... _____
         _____

13 20...... _____
         _____

20...... _____
         _____

20...... _____
         _____

20...... _____
         _____

20...... _____
         _____

14 20...... _____
         _____

20...... _____
         _____

20...... _____
         _____

15

20....... _____

_____

20....... _____

_____

20....... _____

_____

20....... _____

_____

20....... _____

_____

16

20....... _____

_____

20....... _____

_____

20....... _____

_____

20....... _____

_____

20....... _____

_____

OCTOBER

20...... _____
_____

20...... _____
_____

17 20...... _____
_____

20...... _____
_____

20...... _____
_____

20...... _____
_____

20...... _____
_____

18 20...... _____
_____

20...... _____
_____

20...... _____
_____

19

20......

20......

20......

20......

20......

20

20......

20......

20......

20......

20......

OCTOBER

20...... _____
_____

20...... _____
_____

21 20...... _____
_____

20...... _____
_____

20...... _____
_____

20...... _____
_____

20...... _____
_____

22 20...... _____
_____

20...... _____
_____

20...... _____
_____

20...... _____
_____
20...... _____
_____
23 20...... _____
_____
20...... _____
_____
20...... _____
_____

20...... _____
_____
20...... _____
_____
24 20...... _____
_____
20...... _____
_____
20...... _____
_____

OCTOBER

20....... _____
_____

20....... _____
_____

25 20...... _____
_____

20...... _____
_____

20...... _____
_____

20...... _____
_____

20...... _____
_____

26 20...... _____
_____

20...... _____
_____

20...... _____
_____

27 20......

20......

20......

20......

20......

20......

28 20......

20......

20......

20......

20......

OCTOBER

20...... _____
_____

20...... _____
_____

29 20...... _____
_____

20...... _____
_____

20...... _____
_____

20...... _____
_____

20...... _____
_____

30 20...... _____
_____

20...... _____
_____

20...... _____
_____

31

20......

20......

20......

20......

20......

NOVEMBER

NOVEMBER

20...... _____

20...... _____

1 20...... _____

20...... _____

20...... _____

20...... _____

20...... _____

20...... _____

2 20...... _____

20...... _____

20...... _____

20...... _____
_____
20...... _____
_____
3 20...... _____
_____
20...... _____
_____
20...... _____
_____

20...... _____
_____
20...... _____
_____
4 20...... _____
_____
20...... _____
_____
20...... _____
_____

NOVEMBER

20 ...... _____
   _____

20 ...... _____
   _____

5 20 ...... _____
   _____

20 ...... _____
   _____

20 ...... _____
   _____

20 ...... _____
   _____

20 ...... _____
   _____

6 20 ...... _____
   _____

20 ...... _____
   _____

20 ...... _____
   _____

20......

20......

7 20......

20......

20......

20......

20......

8 20......

20......

20......

185

NOVEMBER

9

20...... _____
         _____

20...... _____
         _____

20...... _____
         _____

20...... _____
         _____

20...... _____
         _____

20...... _____
         _____

10

20...... _____
         _____

20...... _____
         _____

11

20......
20......
20......
20......
20......

12

20......
20......
20......
20......
20......

NOVEMBER

20...... _____

_____

20...... _____

_____

13 20...... _____

_____

20...... _____

_____

20...... _____

_____

20...... _____

_____

20...... _____

_____

14 20...... _____

_____

20...... _____

_____

20...... _____

_____

20...... _____

20...... _____

15 20...... _____

20...... _____

20...... _____

20...... _____

20...... _____

16 20...... _____

20...... _____

20...... _____

NOVEMBER

20...... _____

20...... _____

17 20...... _____

20...... _____

20...... _____

20...... _____

20...... _____

18 20...... _____

20...... _____

20...... _____

19 20......
20......
20......
20......
20......

20 20......
20......
20......
20......
20......

NOVEMBER

20...... _____
          _____

20...... _____
          _____

21 20...... _____
          _____

20...... _____
          _____

20...... _____
          _____

20...... _____
          _____

20...... _____
          _____

22 20...... _____
          _____

20...... _____
          _____

20...... _____
          _____

20......

20......

23 20......

20......

20......

20......

20......

24 20......

20......

20......

NOVEMBER

20...... _____

20...... _____

25 20...... _____

20...... _____

20...... _____

20...... _____

20...... _____

26 20...... _____

20...... _____

20...... _____

27　20......

20......

20......

20......

20......

28　20......

20......

20......

20......

20......

NOVEMBER

20...... _____

20...... _____

29 20...... _____

20...... _____

20...... _____

20...... _____

20...... _____

30 20...... _____

20...... _____

20...... _____

DECEMBER

DECEMBER

20...... _____
_____

20...... _____
_____

| 20...... _____
_____

20...... _____
_____

20...... _____
_____

20...... _____
_____

20...... _____
_____

2 20...... _____
_____

20...... _____
_____

20...... _____
_____

3 20......

20......

20......

20......

20......

4 20......

20......

20......

20......

20......

DECEMBER

20...... _____

_____

20...... _____

_____

5 20...... _____

_____

20...... _____

_____

20...... _____

_____

20...... _____

_____

20...... _____

_____

6 20...... _____

_____

20...... _____

_____

20...... _____

_____

7

20...... _____
_____
20...... _____
_____
20...... _____
_____
20...... _____
_____
20...... _____
_____

20...... _____
_____
20...... _____
_____

8

20...... _____
_____
20...... _____
_____
20...... _____
_____

DECEMBER

9

20...... _____
_____
20...... _____
_____
20...... _____
_____
20...... _____
_____
20...... _____
_____

10

20...... _____
_____
20...... _____
_____
20...... _____
_____
20...... _____
_____
20...... _____
_____

11

20......

20......

20......

20......

20......

12

20......

20......

20......

20......

20......

DECEMBER

13

20......

20......

20......

20......

20......

14

20......

20......

20......

20......

20......

15

20......

20......

20......

20......

20......

16

20......

20......

20......

20......

20......

DECEMBER

20...... _____
          _____
20...... _____

17 20...... _____
          _____
20...... _____
          _____
20...... _____
          _____

20...... _____
          _____
20...... _____
          _____

18 20...... _____
          _____
20...... _____
          _____
20...... _____
          _____

19

20......

20......

20......

20......

20......

20

20......

20......

20......

20......

20......

DECEMBER

21

20...... _____

20...... _____

20...... _____

20...... _____

20...... _____

22

20...... _____

20...... _____

20...... _____

20...... _____

20...... _____

23

20...... _____

20...... _____

20...... _____

20...... _____

20...... _____

24

20...... _____

20...... _____

20...... _____

20...... _____

20...... _____

DECEMBER

20...... _____

_____

20...... _____

_____

25 20...... _____

_____

20...... _____

_____

20...... _____

_____

20...... _____

_____

20...... _____

_____

26 20...... _____

_____

20...... _____

_____

20...... _____

_____

27 20......

20......

20......

20......

20......

28 20......

20......

20......

20......

20......

DECEMBER

20...... _____
_____

20...... _____
_____

29 20...... _____
_____

20...... _____
_____

20...... _____
_____

20...... _____
_____

20...... _____
_____

30 20...... _____
_____

20...... _____
_____

20...... _____
_____

31

20......

20......

20......

20......

20......